Being Your Mama

Written by ASHLEY PERROTTI
Illustrated by FAZAL NABBIE

Archway Publishing books may be ordered through booksellers or by contacting:

Archway Publishing
1663 Liberty Drive
Bloomington, IN 47403
www.archwaypublishing.com
844-669-3957

Interior Image Credit: Fazal Nabbie

ISBN: 978-1-6657-2545-3 (sc)
ISBN: 978-1-6657-2546-0 (hc)
ISBN: 978-1-6657-2544-6 (e)

Print information available on the last page.

Archway Publishing rev. date: 07/29/2022

To my daughters,

Thank you for making me a mama.

To my mother,

Thank you for showing me
how to be a great one.

Being your mama means waking up with a reason.

And that means forever, not just a day, month, or season.

Being your mama means seeing tiny little bits of myself in you.

It may be on your face, in your words, or something that you do.

Being your mama means picking up your toys.

Not once, not twice, not three times, MORE!

Being your mama means cutting your waffle into tiny little chunks.

Sometimes you eat it, sometimes you don't, and sometimes it becomes my lunch.

Being your mama means opening the back of your diaper to peek in.

Pee-yew! That's a stinky one. Off to the diaper bin!

11

Being your mama means buying you a new dress.

I buy yours before mine, to make sure you look your best!

Being your mama means begging you to take your first steps.

Then once you start, you don't stop, so there's never a rest!

Being your mama means being more excited for your birthday than mine.

The presents, the pictures, your smile.
It's worth it every time!

Being your mama means I look at Daddy
in a different way.

Before you my love, he wasn't a Daddy,
and all that changed in one day!

Being your mama means I look at Grandma different too.

Now I know what it takes to be a mommy,
and I see what she's been through.

Being your mama means my heart hurt
your first time at daycare.

You're growing up before my eyes, and it's a lot for a mom to bear.

Being your mama means it's hard when we're away.

When you're back in my arms, it's the best part of my day!

Being your mama means
everything to me.

You are my whole wide world, and forever my baby you'll be.

Printed in the United States
by Baker & Taylor Publisher Services